# ANCHOR BOOKS

EXPRESSED EMOTIONS

Edited by

Rachael Radford

First published in Great Britain in 2003 by
ANCHOR BOOKS
Remus House,
Coltsfoot Drive,
Peterborough, PE2 9JX
Telephone (01733) 898102

All Rights Reserved

Copyright Contributors 2003

HB ISBN 1 84418 096 4
SB ISBN 1 84418 097 2

FOREWORD

Poetry has become more and more popular over recent years - with people choosing to write poems in order to unchain feelings and emotions. This special anthology of poetry, *Expressed Emotions,* acts as a platform for both new and established writers to share their work with a wider audience.

The chosen subjects of the writers vary but they use their creativity to the full in order to share views and pass on thought-provoking messages. The poems are easy to relate to and encouraging to read, offering engaging entertainment to their reader.

This delightful collection is sure to win your heart, making it a companion for life and perhaps even earning that favourite little spot upon your bookshelf.

Rachael Radford
Editor

CONTENTS

Happiness Is	Natasha Yogaratnam	1
Motivation	Douglas Bryan Kennett	2
Happy Tears	Sarah Blackmore	4
Happiness	Marlene Allen	5
Middlewood Way	Olive Torkington	6
My Happiness	Pat Heppel	7
Cloud Nine (Sonnet)	Olliver Charles	8
Nostalgia	Sylvia Partridge	9
Polish Yer! Bike	Paul Volante	10
Happiness Is Me	Carol Ann Darling	11
New Home	Susan Shaw	12
Happiness	David Sheasby	13
Zoom	R Tweedy	14
90 Today	I Jerome	15
Happiness Is	Kathleen McBurney	16
Happiness Is . . .	Peggy Hemmings	17
Happiness Is An Operation Called A Laparascopic . . .	Jackie Stubington	18
Untitled	Dale Finlay	19
State Of Mind	Sylvia Riley	20
True Happiness	Alma Montgomery Frank	21
The Rain	Mary Shepherd	22
Ode To Rain	Elizabeth Morton	23
The Manor House	Helen King	24
Shopping In The Rain	Ivy Allpress	25
A Farmer's Lament	Marie Wood	26
The Deserted Street	Arthur Pickles	27
The Stranger At The Lights	Gail Sturgess	28
Moorland Rain	R Bowhill	29
Spider In The Bath	Henry Rayner	30
Age	Wendy Walker	31
A Portrait Of Life	Pauline Wardle	32
The Teeth Lifter	Toni Attew	33
Poor Cow	Robert Burden	34
My Favourite Poem	Lachlan Taylor	35

Title	Author	Page
Rain At Last	Charlotte Clare	36
Christmas Time	Sheila Buckingham	37
The Man From Ealing	Jean P McGovern	38
Feelings	Kayleigh-jo .Brittain	39
That Crazy Old Game	Steven Krzymowski	40
Slices Of My Happiness Cake	Ethel Oates	41
Since Age	Joan Prentice	42
The Bully	Amanda Leighton	43
No Fuss About Gus	Ray Boyce	44
Something Better Perhaps	Finlay Campbell	46
For Ladies Only	Angela Helen	47
Ghost Town	John Smurthwaite	48
Learner's Nightmare Number One	Claire Daniels	49
The Arrival Of North Sea Gas 14/1/74	Thelma Jean Cossham Everett	50
A Summer Morn	I T Hoggan	51
Hovels To Hi-Tech	Paddy Jupp	52
I Wish	D Parry	54
Reflections	Rosalind Wood	55
The Door	David Gahan	56
Reclaim Your Happiness	Andrea Darling	57
Two Men Talking In Outer Space	Helen Dick	58
Eric, The Electric Cat	Janet Miotti	59
My Dogs	B Lamus	60
Six New Hats	Joan Wylde	61
A Fete Worse Than Death	Jim Potter	62
Knitting!	Maureen Ayling	63
Tomorrow	Dorothy Elthorne-Jones	64
A Lady Who Lived In North Riding	Norma Rudge	65
Idle Thoughts	Betty Nevell	66
Short Skirt	Wendy Davison	67
The Church Fete	M Murray	68
10	J A Brown	69
Mixed Brew	R Vincent	70
Flu 2000	Katherine Parker	71

The Phantom Caster	Evelyn Balmain	72
The Tale Of The Hoghton Elves	Margaret B Baguley	73
The Homesick Sailor	Roger Williams	74
Two Christmas Limericks	Peter English	75
The Nightmare	May Ward	76
God's Reminder	Steffen Ap Lloyd	78
A Summer's Evening	Doreen Petherick Cox	79
Starlings	D A Davies	80
The Gentleman	Aleene Hatchard	82
You Traitor!	Judith Kemp	83
Masquerade	Raymond Spiteri	84
In A Portuguese Restaurant	Irene Roberts	85
The Immortals	Robert Allen	86
Partly Sighted	T Sexton	87
An Idea, A Glint, Passable To Print?	Dennis Overton	88
Dreams Of Night	Leonie Lewis Park	90
Play That Place Again	Joyce Atkinson	91
What Is Happiness?	Joyce Reeves Holloway	92
Love The Second Time Around	Kathleen Stokes	93
Happiness	Janet Bowen	94
Remembering Kindness	Ann Nunan	95
Rain, Rain, Rain	J Feaviour	96
In Another Man's World	Davide A Bermingham	97
Torrential Rain	Doreen M Bowers	98
Rain	Rose Mills	99
An Ode To 'The Yobbo'	Andrew V Ascoli	100
Autumn Days	Allan McFadyean	101
The Lack Of Rain!	Reg Anderson	102
Untitled	Trudy Simpson	103
To Dream The Dream	Sheila E Harvey	104
Happiness Is	J Moore	105
Autumn Cheer	Kathy Rawstron	106
The Meaning Of True Happiness	Robert Doherty	107
A Norfolk Landscape	A M Craven	108
Happy Holidays!	V M Archer	109
Happiness Is . . .	Beryl M Malkin	110

Feelings	Barbara Tunstall	111
Golf Crazy	Dennis Young	112
Happiness Is . . .	Lydia M Storey	114
The Betting Shop	Gerard Chamberlain	115
Another World	Rosemary Mortimore	116

HAPPINESS IS

Blue sky, white clouds
On a bright, sunny day,
A picnic by
A swan filled lake,
The glorious colours
Of a sunset.

Snuggling up in a
Warm, cosy bed,
Time to call your own,
To do whatever you want,
The scrumptious taste
Of chocolate.

Chilling out in front of the TV,
Watching your favourite programme,
Soaking your cares away in the soapy suds
Of a nice, hot bath,
Closing your eyes and dreaming
You were somewhere else.

Laughing and joking
With friends,
Knowing that someone loves you
And always will,
Knowing that you love someone
And always will!

Natasha Yogaratnam

MOTIVATION

What drives you on, shy, little boy
As you sit alone at play
With your ever improving Meccano toy?
- 'What patience,' did Grandma say.

What drives you on at eleven plus
As you work so hard at school?
Is it because it would cause a fuss
To fail and feel a fool?

What drives you on in early teens
As you work and seldom play?
Is it because there aren't the means
For that blazer - just Sunday grey?

What drives you on in later teens
As skills begin to show?
Is it because of foggy dreams
You want to cause to grow?

What drives you on at college
And away from its social life?
Is it the vital need for knowledge
And the best for your future wife?

What drives you on to go abroad
And there to work so hard?
Is it to rise above the herd
And have garden replace backyard?

What drives you on to strive and rise
Through tough industrial scenes?
For now you are more worldly wise
And have yourself more means.

What drives you on to perfect a yacht
With hours apart alone?
For wealth in part you now have got
And loving wife at home.

What drives you on to sail the seas
And seek a distant shore?
Is it now to be at ease,
Not gobble life as before?

What must drive you now is today, not tomorrow,
- For life's transience now you know.
Time was never there to borrow;
Share life's riches - but please go slow.

Douglas Bryan Kennett

HAPPY TEARS

Happiness is to be with you,
Upon rare times when love slips through.
Wooed at first by honeyed word,
Naive, believing all I heard.
When ripe I tumbled in your lap,
Then cynically you sprang the trap.
Now I hope 'gainst casual you,
That force of wish will make love true.
But any hint of future plan,
Sees you become all bachelor-man.
At times of bliss I dare not speak
Of tears that sometimes course my cheek.
Can life be happy? Possibly,
That's yes for you - but no for me.

Sarah Blackmore

HAPPINESS

Happiness is having someone who cares,
That special someone with whom one shares
One's hopes and dreams, laughter and tears,
Enjoying life together, allaying any fears.

Happiness is a family out for a stroll
With a fine dog who is chasing a ball;
They stop and look around at the scenery.
It is true, the best things in life are free!

Happiness is having a chat with old friends,
Reminiscing on the past, exploring new trends,
Exchanging funny stories, laughter fills the air;
There it is again, that longing to share.

Happiness is greeting everybody with smiles,
Lending a hand to help climb life's stiles.
It seems to me that happiness is simply love,
The love of God that comes from Heaven above.

Marlene Allen

MIDDLEWOOD WAY

Have you ever been along Middlewood Way?
I ride my horse there every day.
Dozens of rabbits hopping about
And even Mr Fox has been seen out.
Birds flying around, cheeping and singing
The sweetest songs you've ever heard.
Fat little robins and pied wagtails a-bobbin,
Chaffinch and goldfinch and bonny blackbird.
Lots of wild flowers, too many to count,
Meadowsweet and trefoil, tufted vetch and agrimony,
Iris and bulrush, foxglove and daisy,
Cranesbill and hawkbit and tall willowherb.
Now here come the grass cutter, chop, chop, chop.
Ah well, let's hope there's a second crop.

Olive Torkington

MY HAPPINESS

My happiness is

Reaching a healthy seventy years
After a long, wonderful life,
Feeling smug with warm contentment
As a beloved mother and wife.
Seeing long-awaiting grandsons
Settling well at primary school,
Proud in their little achievements,
Learning hard work is the rule.

Enjoying early retirement,
Visiting countries far away,
Spending time at home, in the garden,
Relaxing at the end of day.
Starting hobbies long avoided,
Pushed aside during working years,
Knitting, reading, poetry writing,
Safe in God's love, having no fears.

Togetherness with my husband
Enduring fifty golden years,
Spared to see our spastic daughter
Reaching undreamt of adult years,
True happiness is life itself,
Sharing blessings God has given,
Living with patience, joy and love
Knowing sins will be forgiven!

Pat Heppel

CLOUD NINE (SONNET)

The rain from cloud nine falls in slow motion -
Diamonds and pearls on emerald grass.
The splashing puddles stir deep emotion;
Single ruby rose in slender glass.
The jewels around the world's pretty face,
Like a broken necklace, those diamond drops.
The hand of the wind sets them all in place,
From silver-lined clouds, those precious raindrops.
Trinkets and treasures, and many a gem -
Gold sun is setting in the sapphire sky.
Red, yellow and blue jewels on a stem.
Silver moon and platinum stars are high:
A puddle - the moon and stars at my feet,
To pause, and wonder when we will next meet?

Olliver Charles

NOSTALGIA

Days long ago
when we played our childhood games.
The meadow where we sat
and made those daisy chains.
The day that you and I
won the three-legged race.
Then fished for tiny tadpoles
and found not a trace.

Mayday and we made garlands
and posies from the flowers
then trudged around the village
in sudden springtime showers.
Summertime and we would go
for picnics by the sea
dreaming of the people
we, one day, would be.

Days of yesteryear
when we brought the harvest in,
the old rusty harvester
made such an awful din.
The husks from the corn
blew in our eyes and hair
when evening came we wandered
round the autumn cherry fair.

Sunshine days of youth
and then we were growing up.
We threw away our toys
and learnt how to cook.
Picking our own blackberries
from the hedge down the lane,
and said goodbye to schooldays
thro' a mist of tears and rain.

Sylvia Partridge

POLISH YER! BIKE

Polish yer! bike and make it shine
Don't drink the wine.
Just polish yer bike. Why? Because it's all mine.
I love to ride it fast and slow
Even through the snow
In towns and villages ever so slow
So all can see it's aglow
People look and stare because of the
Studs and leather saddle bags all gleaming with delight.
And a radio that sounds out the Colonel Bogie march
I love to ride my motorbike all polished and bright
All 1100cc of it at that
It's a Harley Davidson look-alike
Even when it gives you a fright.
But at night I tuck it in its bed
And wish it goodnight.
I'll tell you what, it's better than a wife.

Paul Volante

HAPPINESS IS ME

Happiness is me,
Always writing poetry,
Or riding my cycle lazily.
Often sitting in the garden in warm sunshine,
Reading or meditating, not watching the time.
A cream cake for tea,
Trips to the sea,
Burning fragrant candles, being with my family.
Painting with oils for hours,
Buying bunches of flowers,
Touching falling snow,
To be by a cosy fire's glow.
Walking for miles,
Giving out smiles,
Happiness is me.

Carol Ann Darling

NEW HOME

Our precious home we did loose so sadly,
Because things had gone so badly,
Over the threshold it had to be,
Many a tear I did shed, for all to see.

Yet Mother so very dear,
You offered us a home so near,
Much kindness did you give,
Where we could live.

But that home wasn't ours to keep,
So sadness in did seep,
A new home we must find,
Be it of a similar kind.

I didn't want again to move,
But you were there to prove,
Joy could be mine again,
Instead of all the inner pain.

Now I love my new home,
With happiness it did come,
Bringing in the light of day,
Which has come with me to stay.

Susan Shaw

HAPPINESS

Happiness is something
That we create in our mind
Not something we search for
And seldom we can find

It is just waking up at
The beginning of the day
By counting all our blessings
When kneeling down to pray

It is giving up thoughts
That breed discontent
And accepting what comes
As a gift that is Heaven sent

It's giving up wishing
For things we have not
And making the best
Of whatever we've got

David Sheasby

ZOOM

Living in the year 2000
Don't think I can keep up with the pace.
My friend Chloe is chatting to a team of robots.
I think she fancies a trip up into space.
Cars, trains, buses have all been barred.
Travel to work in a miniature flying saucer now, it moves through air that fast, sometimes miss out on using my swipe card.
Environment free of pollution
coal, oil, gas to go
replaced with power pack charger.
A week's charge gives you enough power only Samson would know.
Telephones don't ring or bleep anymore, customers are fitted with a digital ear sensor, conversations are easy, not so much a bore.
With advanced technology moving at an alarming rate, employment will suffer although leisure will be great.
Graves, cremations will be a thing of the past, government has fitted everyone with a self destruct button, when you reach 71 you must give it
a blast.
Not complaining, had a fantastic life, been to Mars twice, brought a Martian back for my wife.

R Tweedy

90 TODAY
(Dedicated to Lilian, my mum-in-law, who was 90 on 23rd April 2002)

What a lady, she's 90 today,
so dear and sweet in every way,
she is so excited, happy and bright,
she is waiting to open her
presents full of delight!
Hope she is pleased with what she gets,
most of all the cake
will be such a surprise!
But the thrill will be just great
she will remember it just like
she did when she was eight.

I Jerome

HAPPINESS IS

Happiness can never be all yours or all mine,
A measure of happiness fills or flows to remind.
We treasure each moment and hope it will last,
We can't buy it or own it, it's in the present or past.
Happiness can be tinged with sadness and joy,
Always fragile, always strong, in a man, woman, girl or boy.
When we have it, we feel it, and it shows,
When we are happy our faces radiate a special glow.

Kathleen McBurney

HAPPINESS IS...

It's strange how small things make us happy
It's a most elusive feeling.
Sometimes a smile across a room
Can send our senses reeling.

A walk in a meadow where buttercups grow -
A child's moist hand gripping tight as we go.
A dream of a loved one, a memory past,
A love in life that will always last.

It doesn't need riches or extravagant gestures
If one is content with life's little pleasures.
Don't reach for the moon - or live life in a frenzy,
Or give in to that feeling we know as envy.

Birdsong can lift us up to the skies -
See the wonder in a baby's eyes,
Love them, and every night say, 'God bless'
You'll be tied in the ribbons of happiness.

Peggy Hemmings

HAPPINESS IS AN OPERATION CALLED A LAPARASCOPIC CHOLECYSTECTOMY

Hurray! Hurrah! You'll hear me shout.
Last week I had my gall bladder out.
For months I had been feeling ill,
Which wasn't cured by any pill.
But keyhole surgery did the trick.
Now there's no more pain or feeling sick.
But in my convalescent state,
When there's not much to do 'cept contemplate,
There is one thought that occurred to me.
Did the surgeons use a skeleton key?

Jackie Stubington

UNTITLED

I see it damp, where it was dry,
That's what first caught my eye.
I saw a puddle, forming there,
It's only rain, I didn't care.
Becoming larger, it became a pond,
At this stage I'm not real fond.
Growing still, it became a stream,
Panic stricken, I gave a scream.
Still more rain, now there's a lake,
That's when I began to shake.
There's now a river to the sea,
I was scared, so there's no me.

Dale Finlay

STATE OF MIND

The rain falls like molten diamonds
As it spatters my face from a cloud;
But all that you do with this Heaven-sent gift
Is run and retreat with heads bowed.

    You may think that I've just had a smoke,
    Or been dumb-struck by lightning's swift stroke;
    But let it thunder and roar, too right I don't care
    For my state of mind sees no need for repair.

Yesterday's world was grey and dull,
And there seems no reliable way
Of knowing for certain what tomorrow may bring,
Or what hopes and new colours might say.

    Let them whisper and run in suspicion while heads all around turn
                                                    and twist
    As they ruminate in their narrow minds at occasions that don't
                                                     even exist.
    So let it thunder and roar, for I'm not really minding
    For my state of mind sees no need for defining.

The music of the storm inspires my mind
To thoughts long lost in love and singing glory
And I realise to cope with this existence
I'd have to see the world as one big fairy story.

    You complex people try once again in vain
    To protect yourselves against relentless rain;
    While I pray for thunder and the roar, too right I will not bother
    As my state of mind I finally discover.

Sylvia Riley

TRUE HAPPINESS

True happiness begins in the soul
Filling the whole body with a glow
Feeding it with tender love in a glittering bowl

One's nature is dependent on the happiness within
No matter what may befall
True happiness begins in the soul

Lift up your heart and happiness will thrive
Greeting you with sparkling desires
Feeding it with tender love in a glittering bowl

Let others see your happiness
Shining in your merry face
True happiness begins in the soul

The excitement of knowing great happiness within
Shows in your voice and sets off a merry word for others
Feeding it with tender love in a glittering bowl

Rejoice, rejoice, in the happiness that shines
When all around at once happiness reigns
True happiness begins in the soul
Feeding it with tender love in a glittering bowl

Alma Montgomery Frank

THE RAIN

Storm clouds gather in the sky
Coatless people hurry by
Soon the rain begins to fall
Saturating one and all
Water running down the panes
Gushing out of blocked up drains
Leaves that to the ground did flutter
Sailing swiftly down the gutter
Then at last the sun shines through
But without rain what would we do?

Mary Shepherd

ODE TO RAIN

I like it when it rains
When the wind blows hard against the windowpane
The sound of water rushing along the gutters
Loosening the leaves so down they flutter
Hearing the pit-patter on my brolly
Sometimes the clouds are grey, even melancholy.
The feeling of rain on my skin
Dripping off my nose and chin

I like it when it rains
When the water pours down the windowpane.
When it comes with thunder and lightning
If I'm out it can be quite frightening.
But indoors, safe and looking out, it's exciting
Call me weird but to me it's strangely inviting.
Going out getting soaked to the skin
I can always change when I get in.

I really like it when it rains.

Elizabeth Morton

THE MANOR HOUSE

This enchanting old house set in grounds so refined
far away from the road leaving mayhem behind
the long narrow driveway with trees either side
unfolding their branches to welcome with pride
venturing further towards large oak doors
which open inviting its guests to see more
the decor so splendid retains history
as each floor uniquely displays its glory
the rooms now for functions hold secrets untold
secrets from long ago that will never unfold
the long narrow staircase which servants once used
does pervade through this house whilst remaining from view
now the final delight which is favoured by most
the room which is rumoured to shelter a ghost
the finely draped curtains unveil to expose
a garden of splendour where beauty does grow

Helen King

SHOPPING IN THE RAIN

Rain in sheets, just lashing down,
Every time we go to town.

You can safely take a bet,
We've never had a dry trip yet.

Drips from awnings down our necks,
Turns us into frights and wrecks.

Ruined hair-dos, muddy shoes,
We call this our shopping blues.

And now all the shopping's done,
Would you believe it, here's the sun!

Ivy Allpress

A Farmer's Lament

Whilst other lands are dry and bare
We can only stand and stare
At endless rain, day after day
With flooded road and come what may.
The farmer eyed his fields with sorrow,
For rain is promised for the morrow.
His grain is waiting to be mown,
He curses how the weeds have grown.

When men just worked upon the land
And dug his spuds and beets by hand,
It didn't matter what the weather
They just got wet, but worked together.
To fill the sacks, their only aim
And pray the sun comes out again.

But now machines are standing by
And hoping for another try
To get upon the sodden soil
Another wasted day of toil.
With all this progress made in vain
You can't do aught to stop the rain.

Marie Wood

The Deserted Street

Dark, scabrous stones (dirt collectors)
blackened by smoke and grime,
slated roofs cracked and dishevelled
wooden gutters decaying with time.

Tall, derelict buildings
hug the overhanging sky,
shattered, sightless windows
leaky drainpipes that shower passers-by:

Paving stones worn smooth
by the tread of countless feet,
drains clogged with dirt and rubbish
water flooding the street;

Smooth worn cobbles ravaged by time
battered dustbins standing in line,
no gardens, flowers or trees
only a handful of earth clogging weeds . . .

The street is deserted
the people have moved away,
houses stand bare and empty
no laughing children at play.

Arthur Pickles

THE STRANGER AT THE LIGHTS

He stared at me with surprise
An edge of hostility in his eyes
As though I were quite mad
When all I was, was glad

He'd caught me smiling to myself
And singing a little tune
Not something to do in public
Unless you're a buffoon

I remember it was pouring
Oily puddles everywhere
But I was full of pent up joy
I could not help myself, I swear

You know that feeling of elation
No matter of the situation
Regardless of what you do
It just bursts forth all over you

Gail Sturgess

MOORLAND RAIN

The wind it blew, the rain sliced through
Every living thing that grew
And every creature that breath drew,
The torment of that torrent knew
And even man is glad to wait
Within stone walls and roofs of slate,
To venture out would challenge fate,
Until those lashing squalls abate.

R Bowhill

SPIDER IN THE BATH

There's a great big spider in the bath.
Now don't you laugh!
Fetch a duster quick,
Then drop it over him, does the trick.
Free him in the garden
And he quickly scuttles away,
Threatening to return on the very next day!

Henry Rayner

AGE

What is age, this growing old?
It's just a number, or so I'm told.
How you feel and what you do,
Is really, truly, up to you.

Help yourself to stay on top
By walking, not driving to the shop.
Have a swim or ride a bike,
Or better still, go for a hike.

What you eat is what you are,
Oh now look, leave that chocolate bar.
Crisps and biscuits, pop and fudge,
Will not help your weight to budge.

It's easy to put on, but hard to take off,
Like trying to shift a nasty cough.
You have to have a good strong will,
For as of yet there is no pill.

But in the end it's all worth while,
Look back at pictures with a smile,
You've reached your goal, pounds lighter now,
Questions asked, the big one, 'How?'

Wendy Walker

A Portrait Of Life

A portrait of someone
It could be me or yourself
No one can tell how it turns out
It could be a blaze from Hell
Or a painting of God with angels in flight
No matter how it is, we paint from the light
A photo is the same, expressions we see
In the eyes of the beholder
It could be your or it could be me
A portrait of life we see all around
We paint every picture from the sky or the ground.

Pauline Wardle

THE TEETH LIFTER

There once was an old man who was loved very dear
He had a peculiar habit that was strange but very clear
He had some false teeth, both top and bottom
He needed to have them 'cause his own teeth were rotten
He had trouble with them, they didn't quite fit
They would move about in his mouth every time he bit
The bottom teeth were worse, but he didn't want to stick them in
And this is where his funny habit did begin
He started lifting his teeth, he looked like a monkey
He thought he looked all cool and funky
Everyone would laugh at him, he really looked a fright
They said, 'We will throw those teeth in the bin tonight'
He said, 'I will try and not lift my teeth out anymore'
And as soon as his friends had gone, he was lifting them some more
We help him as much as we can
But I guess he wants to lift his teeth and be a monkey man.

Toni Attew

Poor Cow

Spare a thought for me,
Chewing on my cud,
Tail swishing flies,
Hock deep in mud.
Come the winter fields of green,
Are exchanged for barns of hay;
You ought to be more grateful
For your pint of milk a day.

You ought to be more thankful
For the meat upon your plate,
When I cease producing milk,
This will be my fate.
Meanwhile I keep on grazing,
To postpone that awful date;
Prefer to fill your cereal bowl
Than dress your dinner plate.

There must be more to life,
It beggars all belief,
That I should masticate and ruminate,
Until I'm lowing for relief.
Leaking from my udder,
Distressed and morose;
In this intolerable situation
You'd be downright bellicose.

Robert Burden

MY FAVOURITE POEM

Of all the poems that I have read
    the one I keep inside my head
Is that of Wordsworth's Daffodils,
    when read, my heart with pleasure fills.

The poet here has left nothing out,
    he describes them growing round about
I picture now those lovely flowers
    abloom in fields and shaded bowers.

They set the landscape all alight
    like stars in Heaven on a darkened night
Their stems all waft in the breeze that blows
    in perfect unison in their lines and rows.

This is a lovely picture seen each spring
    the beauty that those flowers can bring
With Wordsworth's poem we understand
    to him he sees a wonderland.

Lachlan Taylor

Rain At Last

You must not keep it off the ground, they say,
But I am keen to greet a rainy day;
I want to see the merry droplets dance
Among my newly-rooting, thirsty plants.

The summer season now winds gently down
And autumn leaves fall dry and crisp and brown.
I've waited week and weary week in vain
For that most precious gift of wholesome rain.

I've carried water buckets many hours
To earn next summer's brilliant show of flowers,
But heavenly rain is something I can't give,
So now I hope the plants will drink and live.

I don't forget that some folk suffer flood,
With farmers' crops lost, washed away in mud -
Of more importance than my flower bed,
The means by which the hungry world is fed.

Charlotte Clare

CHRISTMAS TIME

The smell of turkey cooking
And all sorts of other things
All the preparations
Another Christmas brings

Now to fill the stockings
With lots of lovely treats
Oranges and apples
And tasty chocolate sweets

The little ones all in bed
Hope they are asleep
Better wait a little longer
Just in case they peep

Christmas is a lovely time
Mistletoe and pantomime
Christmas pud our table graces
Wonderment on the children's faces

Relaxing after dinner
Tummies have had enough
Kids pull out their selection box
Where do they put the stuff?

The thought of anymore meals today
Makes me feel quite ill
Maybe I'll just condescend
To take an effervescent pill

With Christmas almost over
It has been lots of fun
I'm glad we have to wait a year
Before another one.

Sheila Buckingham

THE MAN FROM EALING

There was a man from Ealing
Who walked up, and down, on the ceiling
When he looked down
He wore such a frown
And had a really sick feeling

It made him feel sick
For the thought, he was thick
And never again, made this dealing
All through the night
It gave him a fright
And never again, walked on the ceiling.

Jean P McGovern

FEELINGS

I feel like I've been trapped
And left to drown in my tears
With only things as blood-curdling
As my darkest fears

I've been locked away in Hades
I'm suffering silently
I've been longing to get out for ages
I'm acting very violently

Silence is my friend
Violence is the answer
If I scream, shout and bawl
They might get me out before I crash or fall

I want to be out in the open
To breathe in fresh air
And what I'm really hoping
Is people won't stop and stare

To stare at the bruises and scars
Deep within my feelings
Caused by self harm
They never start healing

Emotional bruises and scars
They're from the past
From all the hurt and harm
I hope these feelings won't last

Kayleigh-jo Brittain

THAT CRAZY OLD GAME

Golf is a game which the old Scots created
Where you pay quite a lot to end up frustrated
You work all week as a means to an end
And now that it's Sunday you try to pretend
That the book you have studied will improve your play
And nothing can happen to ruin your day
So with no more ado you settle your fee
Then promptly head off to the very first tee

You slice your first shot, good grief that went wide
The embarrassment starts and there's no place to hide
As you trundle away to where the ball's landed
The catcalls begin, you've already been branded

Now your nerves are on edge so the next shot you rush
Which promptly ends up smack bang in a bush
And despite your best efforts at coaxing the ball
The snail at your feet comes out first at a crawl

The morning goes by with you losing your rag
As you play this new type of game called zigzag
Everyone's ducking and getting irate
As they try to work out if you'll swerve or hit straight

You find every bunker then plop in the swill
Your scorecard now reads like a huge shopping bill
And to top it all off it's started to rain
As you find that your wife's nicked your brolly again

At last you sink the final putt of the day
You don't show your face at the nineteenth, no way!
They've run out of plasters to patch up the bruises
What kind of game's this where everyone loses?

Steven Krzymowski

SLICES OF MY HAPPINESS CAKE

Some slippers and chocolates.
Two tickets for a rugby match.
My cat curled soft upon my lap
While raindrops sing pit-a-pat.
The washing blowing on my clothes line.
A good book and an hour of free time.
Golden daffodils nodding in a gentle breeze
My fruit cake baking that's sure to please.
Bright summer sunshine warming my head.
New comfortable shoes in which to tread.
Snowflakes falling giddy and soundless
Watched through a windowpane.
The laughter of children I know
Who will come to visit again.
Fairy lights sparkling on any Christmas tree
A soft velvet skirt bought especially for me.
To hear the melody of a lovely song
That stirs a memory held strong.
Stories told of years gone by
That make me laugh and also cry.

Ethel Oates

SINCE AGE

Since I've grown older
I'm taking lots of pills
They help me tremendously
Cure all my ills.

Think I've put some weight on
Over all the years
My fat is quite excessive
Then again, who cares?

My wrinkles have wrinkles
My hair is so thin
My eyebrows are thickening
My sight getting dim.

Yet in spite of my ageing
And looking so gross
I'm glad I'm still living
So don't care a toss.

We're all getting older
So age has to be
When we stop getting older
We just cease to be.

Joan Prentice

THE BULLY

The bully is one who ought to be pitied,
By brawn he might win but by brains is outwitted.
He really is fearful of those he condemns,
He boasts a big gang but he has no real friends.

The bully dislikes traits he doesn't possess,
Authentic appeal, refinement, finesse.
No care from his kin and no real discipline,
His ego is huge and his patience is thin.

The bully despises all things that he lacks,
Stealing from others he gets his own back.
At work he is loathed though he has achieved fame,
Folks pull rude faces at the sound of his name.

The bully at night goes on home to his bed,
A fine house and car but no girl has he wed.
Lost and alone, life never brings him much joy,
He's scared as a rabbit, this sad little boy.

Amanda Leighton

No Fuss About Gus

Once upon a time in the West
The local sheriff wore a vest
Made of wool and buffalo hide
Enough to keep him warm inside

His name was Gus - a shotgun man
Any trouble - then bang - a double bang
No robbers or bandidos ever tried
To loot the bank from inside

But one day, an outlaw gang
Robbed the stage with the Ku Klux Klan
Two men dead - the gold box gone
What could Gus do to right this wrong?

A woman also kidnapped from the stage
Provoked the township with outrage
She was young and quite a looker
'Twas Gus's girl, Bezides Booker

The gang leader carried a wooden cross
To show who really was the boss
Cold blue eyes peered through his mask
As he concentrated upon his task . . .

Gus, meanwhile, was in the town
Organising trackers of renown
Fighting men were in this bunch
But didn't leave until after lunch

As the posse passed the stricken stage
Gus was consumed by an inner rage.
Where were the bandits holding his girl
His head was aching - his mind a whirl

Bezides was cold - tied up in a cave
Expecting the worst - trying to be brave
Alone - she screamed with all her might
Enough to bring down a stalactite

'Calcium' Carbonate was a bearded trapper
How she was rescued doesn't much matter
Returned her to town to much local acclaim
Never to be seen or heard of again

Rumour had it that Gus had been killed
By an angry Apache - his liver was grilled
No one knew - no one was sure
One thing for certain - wasn't seen anymore

So outlaws and posse still to this day
May be in hiding a long way away
Looking at it through from a logical angle
They probably vanished in the Texas triangle.

Ray Boyce

Something Better Perhaps

Much better it is to dispose of litter
The very thought drives vandals wild.
Oldies might choose a pint of bitter
Though some prefer a glass of mild.

Is life improved by telephonic faxes?
Clever 'tis true, but not quite magic.
Highly-priced beer is mainly taxes
Political greed is obscenely tragic.

Though struggling manfully to find
Something better now, than of yore,
Probably it would be most unkind
To allege the best has gone before.

Finishing now, concluding sadly,
Modernisers, fat cats and town planners
Promise much yet all fail badly
Not only in content, but in bad manners.

Finlay Campbell

FOR LADIES ONLY

Styled for a lady
With a lady look
It takes four ladies
And a handbook.

With rubber to run on,
The hardness of life,
Four ladies can go along,
No trouble and strife.

They can ease in the warmth
And relax in the comfort,
That ladies can travel
With not too much effort.

With three lazing back
And one doing all,
None of them minding,
Their turn will soon fall.

In darkness they see
By the flick of a switch,
In hail, rain and snow,
They flick that switch.

It runs fairly cheaply,
But cheaper by four.
They all pay together,
The car keeps a store.

The car that I speak of,
The best in a hundred,
Is none other than *the* car,
Triumph Herald 1200.

Angela Helen

GHOST TOWN

Try picturing the way it was . . .
Now a ghost town and all because
S'not economic to use coal
(The only miners left are Poles)
It's lost its people - then its soul
Small businesses have long gone bust
Pits winding gears full of rust
The bowling greens, 'cause they're not mown
Are back to nature overgrown
More like a wildlife sanctuary
Long lost that proud community.

John Smurthwaite

LEARNER'S NIGHTMARE NUMBER ONE

Patience is a virtue some might shout.
But patience can be stretched at a roundabout.
Mile queue behind you, maniacs to the right,
You've been here so long they'll have to call the AA out.

You should have packed a lunch, you've really been here too long,
You know they think you've stalled, but you know they're wrong.
You're starting to portray two of the deadly sins,
Sloth is pretty obvious, but anger is going to win!

The handbrake's yanked, the engine's cranked,
You couldn't get on this roundabout even if you drove a tank,
But you're in a car, so all you can do is pray
For a space on the horizon to come your way.

Yes, you've seen a gap,
Now to make the mad dash,
Foot down on the accelerator,
Oh dear, now your instructor's got whiplash!

Claire Daniels

THE ARRIVAL OF NORTH SEA GAS 14/1/74

This week early, a ring at the bell
For a reason I knew so perfectly well.
I leapt out of bed, my eyes full of sleep
And got to the door to take a peep.
'Have you turned off your gas?' said the young fellow there,
'Oh yes,' I replied without stopping to stare.
From that day on, they worked the whole week
For they knew full well the warmth we would seek.
That job was so real, so I tried all I could
With hot coffee drinks to keep up their zeal.
I helped all I could to clear away mess
And the hot coffee I offered, they said, 'God bless.'
Tonight as they finish and are off and away,
They were still very grateful that during their stay
I'd been there to help them and brighten their day.

Thelma Jean Cossham Everett

A Summer Morn

Like an angelic choir singing,
So the birds are bringing
Music to our ears.
The beauty moves us to tears.
Like music from on high,
So the birds cry,
They sing their praises,
Beauty from the dust raises,
As the sun is born,
On this sweet morn.

I T Hoggan

HOVELS TO HI-TECH

Hovels are mean dwellings,
Our ancestors knew this.
Their tents of wood and hide, their caves
Could hardly have been bliss.

Gradually came mud huts,
Progression through the years.
The men were learning building skills
On many new frontiers.

Different bricks were fashioned
From clay and limestone too,
Some dungs were used and grass as well,
Men's confidence soon grew.

But discontent was brewing
Between the rich and poor.
The serfs' unrest was leading to
The ravages of war.

Nothing much was changing,
The rich man still was king.
Towering castles soon appeared,
A status symbol thing.

Buildings played a big part
In our evolution,
But mankind never seems to learn
That fighting's no solution.

Modern towers, now targets
Are built with glass and steel.
On 11.9.2001
Man's greed was brought to heel.

The world has turned full circle,
Some hi-tech homes today
Are underground, they're safer there,
This century's caves I'd say.

Paddy Jupp

I Wish

'I've won! I've won!' I scream and shout,
The money's mine without a doubt.
A big house, car, cruise holiday,
Some to charity, I'll give some away.

I'll leave my job, pursue my leisure,
Anything I want, it's my pleasure.
I'll treat my friends, have such fun,
My numbers have come up, I really have won.

My heart so happy, a shadow appears,
And to my eyes many tears.
I didn't put on the Lottery,
The dreams in my mind is where they'll be.

D Parry

REFLECTIONS

I look in the mirror
but all I see
is this stranger
staring back at me

Imprisoned
no means of escape
invisible chains
enforce restraint

Watching as life
passes by
always everyone else's
turn to fly

Where is the person
who used to be me?

Waiting to soar
when I am
'set free'

Rosalind Wood

The Door

The door is like a prison trapped deep inside
The door is frustration and a secret kept near
The door is pain and memories of the times I've cried
The door is on fire spitting anger like an inferno of fear
The door is a barrier to high and wide

Words are like ghosts floating on a sea of no meaning
Words are confusing and drift away
Words are spiralling in time in a day of daydreaming
Words are cruel as I stare out of the window on a cold winter day

Writing is like a nightmare, a demon that tortures me
Writing is weakness when you want to be strong
Writing is a world I cannot see
Writing is a life that seems to be wrong

Reading is a book I long to read
Reading is a torment like a razor blade carving me up inside
Reading is a skill we all need
Reading is confusion when I've sometimes lied

The door is a fear that's been overcome
The words are like a thousand armies marching to a war that
                                                                    must be won
Writing is a destiny that must be done
Reading is an adventure of words and a new horizon as I gaze
                                                                    into the sun.

David Gahan

RECLAIM YOUR HAPPINESS!

Why don't we run and skip and play?
Why do we waste our lives away?
Reading bad news on paper every day

Blindly accepting all we're told
To society we are already sold
Like we are cast from the same mould

Slaves to a job we detest
Too soulless to protest
And we wonder why we're depressed

Cut off from nature in concrete misery
Many never see the stars, the sea or a tree
They are just too blind to see

Too busy talking about others over there
We do not consider our own lives of despair
The pain is too much to bear

With all my heart I urge you
Do not let society tear your soul in two
Reclaim your happiness and be born anew

Andrea Darling

TWO MEN TALKING IN OUTER SPACE

The old man said,
'The world goes round at such a pace
I tremble for the human race
And if the speed should get much faster,
The millennium will bring disaster.'

'Well, sir,' said the young man, 'if I were once more below,
I'd do my best to ease the pace, give council to the human race,
For all this speed is not the answer to stopping wars or curing cancer.

All nations should love each other and man would meet man as
                                                    his brother,
Then having put the world to rights,
I'd linger a few more nights,
Just meet a pal, a friend,
A crony, like!
Well, like "Pousie Nan" or "Souter Johnny"
To share a drink and raise our glasses to drink a toast
"Tae the bonny lasses."'

'The world, my son, has never listened,'
And in his eye a sad tear glistened.
'What, me go back? It's hardly likely.
As I said before, son,

It's not bl**dy likely!'

Helen Dick

Eric, The Electric Cat

Eric, The Electric Cat laps his milk
Which makes him fat.
His busy tail with electricity,
He really is a sight to see.

Cunning and smart,
Eric gets ready to make his dart.
Bright and shining eyes,
A powerful beam,
So Eric can see where he has been.

His bed cosy and warm,
No need for central heating,
His electricity keeps his heart beating.
Such a happy cat, full of fun and tricks,
Eric knows we love him to bits.

Janet Miotti

MY DOGS

It is said, a dog is man's best friend,
That saying of course I would like to amend.
Because it is also a woman's privilege to experience that joy,
Indeed, a dog can enhance the lives of a girl or a boy.
With ears alert, tail on the move,
Enquiring eyes just begging to prove
How loyal it can be, faithful and true,
Enforcing that fact when it nudges you.
Offering a paw, wanting to be your friend,
A broken heart it always can help mend.
Giving so much more than it could ever receive,
Do I love my dogs? Yes, indeed.

B Lamus

SIX NEW HATS

'Would it be generous of a man,' asked Jean,
'To buy his wife six new hats then, Dean?'
'It depends,' said he,
On what? asked she.
'If she had seven heads it would seem a bit mean!'

Joan Wylde

A Fete Worse Than Death

It is that time of year
That some people like or hate
This is the moment of fear
'Cause yes, it's Southwood House's fete

Some books and games to buy
Burgers or ices you can eat
With one worried eye on the sky
We hope you won't get wet feet

There's Highland dancing on the menu
Children might try the amazing donkey rides
Tombola and games to play by you
And loads more to do round the sides

So why not come and have some fun
All proceeds go to a good cause
Why not gamble in the sun
The first prize could be yours.

Jim Potter

KNITTING!

I find it so relaxing while I'm sitting in my chair,
To ply the wool and needles and to knit without a care.
Knit 1, purl 1, make 1 - it goes without a hitch
Until I find that suddenly, I've gone and dropped a stitch!

And it's always at the bottom, never at the top -
It makes me very angry and I always have to stop
Whatever I am doing to pick it up again,
I really am beginning to find it quite a pain!

But I find it so relaxing as the needles start to click,
The work's not growing fast enough, I wish the wool was thick!
I'm really getting anxious now, I've dropped it on the mat
And the ball has been unravelled by my playful little cat!

She has captured it and run away, she's having quite a game,
But the ball of wool will never, ever, be just quite the same.
She's wound it round the chair legs and halfway down the hall,
I wish I'd never started to knit this thing at all!

But I find it so relaxing - as an article I make,
Someone will be elated with all the care I take
Whilst knitting them a jumper, or a stocking or a hat,
It really would be quicker without the help of my dear cat!

However, I will persevere and continue with my task
'When will you ever finish it?' I can hear you ask . . .
I've decided, when I'm knitting, that the cat has got to go!
She hinders me in many ways, how much you'll never know.

But I find it so relaxing, with the cat upon my knee,
I think I'll give the knitting up and make a cup of tea!

Maureen Ayling

TOMORROW

Tomorrow must really start to diet
If I'm to get into the model dress,
Foregoing snacks - to keep my conscience quiet,
No longer eating chocolates to excess.

Tomorrow I'll have nothing alcoholic,
In healthy exercise I will engage,
Soon on the lawn with cartwheels I will frolic;
Perhaps my antics will become the rage?

Tomorrow in the garden I'll get busy,
With hoe and rake, with shears and fork and spade;
I'll work till fingers fail and brain is dizzy
Before I sit a moment in the shade!

To guests, however, who are soon expected,
I must true hospitality display,
And so my resolutions are rejected,
To be pursued - perhaps - another day!

Dorothy Elthorne-Jones

A Lady Who Lived In North Riding

A lady who lived in North Riding
Caused chaos by always colliding
She went up to Mars
And collided with stars
So on Jupiter now she's residing!
There was a Welsh farmer from Bala
Who wanted to build a new parlour
His cows got confused
And to milk they refused
Unless he played music from Mahler!
A pirate who found a gold treasure
Had forgotten to learn how to measure
He filled up his boat
Which no longer could float
On the seabed he now spends his leisure!
A man who loved going to shows
Used to sniff at the scent of a rose
One day a queen bee
Which he first failed to see
Stung him right on the end of his nose!
There was a young major from Cork
Who ordered a meal of roast pork
He ate stuffing with dill
But could not pay the bill
And got chased with a fork to New York!
There was a young lady from Rhyl
Who found looping the loop a great thrill
While flying on high
In her plane in the sky
Saw that Snowdon was more than a hill!

Norma Rudge

IDLE THOUGHTS

I think I envy Mr Snail
Protected from the rain and hail

And as for poor old Mr Worm
He can only slide and squirm

Life is hard for Mr Ant
Who has no time to be gallant

But the butterfly is full of colour
Unlike the moth who's so much duller.

Betty Nevell

SHORT SKIRT

Short skirt
What a flirt
Pulling it down
With such a frown
Ill at ease
Trying to make it reach her knees
Tight top
What a flop
Permanently re-adjusting
Seams nearly busting
Fingers running through her hair
Tossing it around like a wild mare
It must be such a pain
When you're so vain.

Wendy Davison

THE CHURCH FETE

The day started sunny the weather was fine
The marquee and stalls were erected
The members of the Ladies Guild
Had their Chairperson duly elected

She directed the ladies with cakes by the ton
Home made jam and pickles in pt
To the tent where the judging
Of these would take place
On one table they put all the lot

Then Mrs McKenzie came waltzing in
Her pet poodle Fifi on a lead
When Mrs McDonald's Alsatian decided
That Fifi would make a good feed

So he chased her up and over and round
The cakes, jams and pickles piled high
The Minister's wife looked on aghast
As the goodies all started to fly

The Scouts, Guides and Brownies
All gathered around
Anxious to help, but no way
The Minister stood with his hands on his head
And didn't know quite what to say

The Brownies by this time were helpless
And rolling all over the place
The Guides tried hard to keep giggles in
The captain to keep a straight face

The Scouts of course were doing their best
To keep quiet, suppress the snigger
As he stood looking on a the chaos around
'Oh bloomin' Hell,' said the Vicar.

M Murray

10

Beneath the boughs of maple trees,
The pathway thick with snow,
And breath a cloud upon the leaves,
Steps silent as they go.
Further into speechless wood,
With all the world asleep,
Sun dimly lit upon the hood,
Ice fairies melt and weep.

The lake lies still in hidden glass,
No movement on its shore,
As bundled soldiers march and pass
Through winter's solemn door.
Their movements muffled in the air,
No destination near,
Our thoughts of laughter do not dare,
Our eyes abject with fear.
We see them as they round the bend
And disappear from sight,
This slice through winter will not mend
Nor stop at piercing night.
They march perhaps to distant shores
Not knowing that we hide,
Watching them through shields of gorse
And wait for eventide.

In springtime blooms will cast their shade
Upon this very spot.
Forgetting paths this army made,
Also, tho, we shall not,
But keep with us through childhood years,
As youngsters often do,
Buried in our deepest fears,
The army marching through.

J A Brown

Mixed Brew

There once was a witch
   who lived in a ditch
and brewed her brews in the hedges.
   She gathered some dank
from the deepest bank
   and some from the edges.

She practised her charms
   by waving her arms
and muttering words and curses;
   and every spell
would have worked out well
   if she hadn't mixed the verses.

Not long since,
   when she wanted a prince
to wake the sleeping beauty
   a man appeared
with a long grey beard
   to old to report for duty!

When she hoped to save
   Aladdin's cave
from his uncle cruel and cranky,
   she concocted a spell
that somehow fell
   not on him, but on Widow Twanky.

With a magic bean
   she called for a queen
who was locked in the wizard's castle;
   there came an old hag
with a postman's bag
   and three pence to pay on the parcel!

R Vincent

FLU 2000

Did you know that a cold came from outer space?
It travels up your astronose
round your eyes and then explodes
just like a meteor showering gloom upon your face.

It's Flu 2000 all the papers say
stay at home, don't go out, then it'll go away.
The thing that puzzles me is
how do they know how many miles it's travelled so
2000 miles is not a long way to travel
just to spoil someone's day.

Well I'm telling it - no cold's getting me
I'm off to play, just you see
whilst others who can't go out of doors
snap and growl, howl and moan
and spoil that day of yours.
I'm off out even in a storm
forgetting the woolly to keep me warm

Oh what's this I see a runny nose - it cannot be
around the world Flu 2000's flown with ease
I think I'm . . . I'm . . . I'm . . . developing a sneeze

So now it's plain for all to see
that Flu 2000 has flown to me.

Katherine Parker

THE PHANTOM CASTER

At nine she's into fishing
Casting and reeling with the best.
Everybody's wishing
That she'd stayed home to rest.
Early morning tide is high,
She changes and tumbles downstairs.
Is it feather? Will it be fly?
As long as it's bait, who cares?
At present she'll be spinning,
Throwing bright metal in the sea.
But she's not going to be winning
Not even a sprat for tea.
'It's a nest! No! It's her line!'
She cast across everyone's path.
But the question is, 'Which line's mine?'
Other fishers ask in wrath.
'The Phantom Caster is here,'
Said one youngster who saw her aim.
But whatever you say my dear,
You must admit she's quite game!

Evelyn Balmain

THE TALE OF THE HOGHTON ELVES

Two men went out one moonlit night and walked to Hoghton Brow.
Said one of them, 'This is the place to catch some rabbits now.
We've got our sacks to carry them, so we will lay a snare.
There's lots or rabbit holes round here, we're sure to catch them there.
The rabbits will come out to feed because the moon is high
And it is almost certain that we'll get our rabbit pie.'

They pegged their sacks across two holes, then went away to wait
Among the trees and bushes tall, that grew beside the gate.
Soon both their sacks were wriggling and jumping all about,
Said one man to the other, 'There isn't any doubt that we've caught two
fine rabbits.
We'll take our sacks and run before the gamekeeper comes out to chase
us with his
gun.'

They slung the sacks upon their backs and went up Hoghton Brow.
A little voice came from a sack, 'Dick, where've tha got to now?'
'I'm in a sack and on a back, I'm having such a ride.'
'Me too, we're going up Hoghton Brow,' another voice replied.

The men just dropped their sacks and ran, they'd had a dreadful fright.
They only came a-creeping back when it was first daylight.
They found their sacks all folded up beside the Tower wall.
They picked them up and shook them out and one of them let fall.
A little note that told them all they should have known themselves,
The ones who played that trick on them were two wee Hoghton elves.

Margaret B Baguley

The Homesick Sailor

One day a ship put out to sea;
A grand old sailing ship was she,
Containing just the crew and me.

I was the captain of that crew;
We'd planned such deeds of derring-do
As never would occur to you.

Just after we had raised the sails,
A helicopter brought the mail;
One letter to the mast was nailed.

It was a message to the crew:
'Forget those deeds of derring-do;
Keep land in sight - I like the view.
(Signed) Captain!'

Roger Williams

TWO CHRISTMAS LIMERICKS

A certain wise man on a camel,
Complained of this curious mammal;
Its contours severe
Gave him pains in the rear,
So he coated himself with enamel!

As shepherds lay close to their fires,
Some angels came winging in choirs;
As they hovered on high
One old man gave cry -
'It's amazing! You can't see the wires!'

Peter English

THE NIGHTMARE

It was on a Friday morning we saw a bathroom suite,
In this shop up Stockwell Street,
It was called Honeymoon, it looked so nice in there,
Believe me it was no honeymoon it became a nightmare.

The cistern had no hole in it where there should have been one,
So off we went to Midco to get a temporary float,
It made a funny noise we hadn't reckoned on,
I can tell you it was better living on a boat.

Soon after I decided to try it out,
Once I got in I did a somersault trying to get out.
The handles are not in the middle,
So that really caused me to shout.

Then the bath started leaking and the floor was all wet,
Geoff came and fixed it and then we were set.
We were okay for a week or so and then the floor was wet again,
This time it was the toilet - oh what a pain!

The toilet had a hole in the bottom believe it or not,
So we rang the firm and told them what we had got.
They said, 'We will send you another as soon as we can.'
Early next morning came a man with a van.

So one toilet delivered, great, whacko!
But they had not sent the cistern; it wasn't all there,
Early next morning there came another knock
Same man, same van, 'Sorry we thought it was out of stock.'

So off we went for Geoff the plumber man,
He said, 'I will come and fix it as soon as I can.'
So Geoff came and fixed it and it was all right
Now we keep our fingers crossed in case of another plight.

So up to now we hope everything will be okay,
If not we will definitely rue the day,
I have come to the end of my bathroom tale,
Oh please let me have a week on the Broads for a peaceful sail!

May Ward

God's Reminder

When you've been rejected
by the one you love,
the pain that you encounter
is sent from God above.
For it's His reminder
that the love that he has lent,
is a gift from Heaven to you
and for abuse it was not meant.
The pain is like no other
and on Earth you will not find,
for it destroys your body
and it clouds your mind.
Your heart's destroyed beyond repair
and the pain inside beyond compare.
For it's God's reminder
that true love you must share.
So please listen to me
for I know it all first hand,
for I have suffered truly
now with no woman do I stand.

Steffen Ap Lloyd

A Summer's Evening

I sit alone in the gardens overlooking the sea.
Now the sun is setting, tinging with purple the
edges of lofty white clouds above me.
My eyes no longer constrained by the sun's piercing rays.
The honeysuckle throws out its perfume, while swaying
gently in the breeze.
I'm so content watching he ships sailing out to sea.

Doreen Petherick Cox

STARLINGS

The swish of the cloud as it sweeps around,
Darkens the sky, until they rain to the ground.
Bobbing and flitting, an ocean of sound,
Millions of pilots, their resting places found.
Fuelling and resting, this carpet of flight,
Fields of excitement the throng of delight.
Posts and telephone wires filled with their verse,
The lookout watching, danger's nurse.

Why do they gather and display in this way?
Starlings so common, weave this wondrous display.
Field full of movement, and then the brush of the air,
The surge of their movement, dances and dares.
Autumn shedding and gathering a farewell,
Winter's troubles and struggles will tell.
The ball and gown, black and brown,
Roaming and raiding, chasing the crown.

They chatter, chirp and chatter, sing, legions or few,
Flowing and drifting, trespassing, laying carpets new.
Rising in an angry wave, surfing the sky,
Rush in the wind, by this cloud gliding by.
They swirl, swivel and turn like a waltz on the wing,
Movement stretching and turning, harmonising
Then returning to fill trees, as though with leaves,
Rustling and ringing, clouds to deceive.

Snowflakes, flitting, blankets their home,
Hiding their kitchen, and the places they roam.
These cheeky chaps with speckled breasts,
Like medals for braving winter's vest.
In groups of melodies, beg on winter's knees,
The bow of the tree, filled respectfully, please.

The filling of the sky with friends in flight,
The stars in the sky
The starlings fly,
High.

D A Davies

THE GENTLEMAN
(A fable of good manners)

'Good day to you, Hare,'
The tortoise said,
As he lifted his shell as he passed.
'You'll never get anywhere sitting there, m'dear,
But you'll certainly come in last!'

The hare didn't respond
But crinkled her eyes,
Gazing down at the grass at her feet.
What a blundering fool he is, she thought,
Yet forever our destinies meet!

'Top of the morning,
A beautiful day,
The race is about to begin.'
The tortoise was sagely nodding his head,
For he knew he could always win.

And the tortoise displayed
His enigmatical smile,
As the hare loped ecstatically past,
For everyone knew that he could have won,
Instead of coming in last!

For every year
He had won that race
And left all the others behind,
But this year he'd felt it only polite
Deciding his place in his mind.

'For you see,' he addressed
All those who were there,
And displayed his full knowing grin,
'A gentleman will always slow down
And let a fair lady win.'

Aleene Hatchard

You Traitor!

I hate you, little alarm clock!
Your hearty morning call
The way you make my heart shake
The way you shout and bawl.

I hate you, little alarm clock!
The way you chose today,
To take some well-earned time off
And not come out to play.

You see my boss has had it
With all my tales of woe,
Of how you just betray me
He says that I must go.

I'm sure I'd learn to love you
If you were just more quiet,
And learnt to never skive work
Or else cause such a riot!

Judith Kemp

MASQUERADE

She pranced about in her long velvet skirt
And showed off in her yellow silk shirt
With titian coloured curly wig to match
She knew, her man she'll catch.

She wasn't worried what people would say
She was enjoying life, come what may
She felt so happy, she'd done it now
When men saw her they raised their brow.

She tried to wiggle and to sway
As through the crowds she made her way
People were dancing in the street
She could not join them, her high heeled shoes hurt her feet

Her wig was too warm on her head
And her skirt too tight, made her feel bad
Her buttons began to pop off her shirt
By end of day she'd seized to flirt
Feeling a right old twerp!

She felt pleased her dream had come true
It was something she always wanted to do
She didn't realise it was so tough
And now she had really had enough
Next carnival time, she'd be herself . . . a man!

Raymond Spiteri

IN A PORTUGUESE RESTAURANT

I went on holiday about a year ago
and as you do, to the toilet I had to go
it was one of these shacks out at the back
because inside the space they did lack

I found the door and gave it a tug
nothing happened, aha it must be stuck
so I pulled harder and it opened a crack
I looked in and oh dear, a face looked back
she perched ashen face and stared at me
exposed as she was for all to see
'Excuse me,' I muttered and hurried away
I couldn't stop laughing for the rest of the day.

Irene Roberts

The Immortals

Have I slept through all those years,
or was it but the blinking of an eye?
The same old television shows,
with same cast, but now more lined and grey.
Do such people never fade away and die?

In my youth I once aspired
to join this happy, immortal band
of radio and television presenters.
At that time my verse never scanned;
I was condemned and damned.

Now I too am past my best,
with thinning hair and old age pension.
No longer do I pester editors and producers.
Confined within these walls I listen
to my fellow oldies grammatic declension.

If I am condemned to hell,
Lord, permit me to escape the chair
in which sits the gentleman
controlling serious debate and discussion
with pointing finger, at 'The Woman Over There'.

Robert Allen

PARTLY SIGHTED

My brother Mick and myself are just that
Faces are misty we cannot see them, a fact
Folk come up to us both and ask us if we know
Themits possible have known them, that's so
For quite some time but being partly sighted
That speaks for itself, yes folk, enough said
I will give you an instance of what my brother Mick did the other day
This did occur whilst out in his buggy, this had to be true
In his road and near his home has a habit you bet
Of saying good morning to folk, no threat
Mick was passing a garden, he said, 'Good morning, OK?'
No answer came, so brother Mick went on his way
On returning from doing a bit of shopping no delay
In that said garden a cement mixer stood that day
Then it came to him that was the reason why no answer
Came from the cement said mixer that did occur.

T Sexton

An Idea, a Glint, Passable To Print?

My A4 pad has been sitting unused, a pen has not visited for some time,
Awaiting subject matter to register, reflect concept, notion, into rhyme.
For energy to transmit, relay impulses forming activity, sensation,
                                                                    in my brain,
A respectable standard of thought to acquire, achieve, attain.
At the precise moment I'm not certain how this muse unfolds, what
                                                               follows next,
No need to seek out a term to explain my current state, one fitting
                                                              is perplexed.
Why not simply switch on the telly, radio, play some music, watch
                                                              a video tape
Some compulsive drive within requires nourishment, offers no escape.
I don't crave attention, wealth, adulation, celebrity, fame or praise,
But like to stimulate interest, break routine, counter lethargic mood,
                                                                  malaise.
Satisfy a need to correspond, relate, converse, impart, communicate,
Build something, accept a challenge, cultivate a purpose, invent, create.
Arrange words, hopefully in an entertaining style, that others wish
                                                                to read,
Once this target has been set, effort, determination are essential to
                                                               succeed.
On completion, assuming my scribble can be deciphered, translated,
It will be 'ink jet imaged', despatched to the editor, and content
                                                              evaluated.
If accepted for an edition, a typeset copy for checking is prepared
                                                             and returned.
Generating euphoric response, and reason for tasks to be temporarily
                                                               adjourned
Reaching this stage involves stamps, stationery, postal service,
                                                             typing prowess,
Professional skills, guidance, supervision, from courteous staff at
                                                             Forward Press.
The poet joins 'kindred spirits' advances to the proud status of
                                                             publication.

When the printer supplies his 'backing', hence promotion, distribution, circulation.
At this juncture, one eagerly wills the mail delivery person to approach the door,
Just like Christmas, a lovely sealed packet, in excitement to handle and explore.
Tearing open carefully reveals an attractive cover, raised to detect our title,
Quality format is admired, digested, as we conduct an impromptu verse recital
Which provides an ego massage, sense of achievement, personal satisfaction,
Incentive to continue writing, fashion a 'lyrical miracle' in future interaction.
Turn the pages, discover gems, shared perspective, well being of self progression
Long may this art form prosper, as contributors unite for a lasting impression.

Dennis Overton

DREAMS OF NIGHT

Cunningly hiding from human eye,
The fairy swordsman of night fly by.
Silently soaring on glistening wings,
Bound for the hall of ancient kings.
Down unseen paths, across the sky,
Legions of swordsmen slip secretly by.

Sounded out on gilded horn,
The fairy call was swiftly borne.
On the eye of the wind from a distant north,
Bringing the fairy swordsmen forth.
They travel towards the coming morn,
Swirling out of the sky in a gleaming swarm.

The call they heard was as old as time,
From the ancient kings who reign sublime.
And the swordsmen know their word is law,
A task will be set they cannot ignore.
So there in the dawn - the air like wine,
The fairy legions wait in line.

Leonie Lewis Park

PLAY THAT PLACE AGAIN

My idea of paradise would be
To take the Proms Orchestra with me
On a luxury world wide cruise
As background music to each setting I choose

Down the world's greatest rivers there would be
A rich baritone serenading me
Expressing the twists and turns life shows
As Old Man River to the sea flows

As mirrored mountains in the fjords reflect
Piano concertos I would select
Vienna at night would be asway
With Strauss waltzes vibrant and gay

For Tangiers, Morocco and Japan
Intriguing themes of that James Bond man
In world capitals and well known beaches
Famous operas to show every depth love reaches

Still half of my paradise keeps returning when
The Proms are on TV again
My chair is exotic places I could be
My transport voice and orchestral harmony

Joyce Atkinson

What Is Happiness?

To be with people that you love,
To share in their pleasures and pain.
Give a helping hand if the need is there
And find this to your gain.

To foster friendship down the years
Sweet memories is the reward.
To embrace the magic of music
To sing praises to the Lord.

Happiness is seeing a smiling face
Or hearing sweet bird song.
Happiness is an outstretched hand
To help one another along.

Happiness is the power of prayer
To soothe the trouble mind.
The all embracing feature
For the benefit of mankind.

Joyce Reeves Holloway

LOVE THE SECOND TIME AROUND

By the church wall we chatted -
Spring sunshine warmed the air.
Grey squirrels played in nearby trees,
Scented flowers lay everywhere.
We felt a kind of comfort -
As we shared a similar past,
Agreed that memories of our loved ones
Would forever last.
We talked about the empty days -
The loneliness of life,
Loss of my dear husband,
And your dear wife.
'Twas then we felt the strangest presence.
Around us from above, as if they smiled upon us -
Understood - and sent their love.
Then from that very moment our lives began anew
Days passed slowly by and we much closer grew.
Now in the twilight of our years -
True happiness we've found
Because we know, in Heaven our love was blessed,
The second time around.

Kathleen Stokes

HAPPINESS

Happiness is walking through dry autumn leaves,
Midst leafy lanes in golden sunlight rays;
The season's colours aglow from bush to tree,
These wondrous patterns only our God weaves.

Happiness is family gath'rings at home,
With Mum in the kitchen
And Dad anxious to help but ne'er bidden;
Jestings and banter, who'd leave this and roam?

Happiness - a candle lit supper for two,
Reminiscing with fond love in their eyes;
Maybe a brisk walk along a sandy shore,
With ebbing tide and seagull calls on cue.

Such pleasures bring happiness beyond measure,
Their cost only time, passing so swiftly;
And we must take the time, while time we still have
To give, and gain happiness in leisure.

Janet Bowen

REMEMBERING KINDNESS

Eaten bread is soon forgotten,
But I've been trained to keep in mind,
Kindnesses, which help to lighten
Burdens, which on my path I find.

I've met such generosity,
From those who stand above the rest,
Who show such sensitivity
When I'm in pain, they are the best.

A loving word from one held dear,
The stranger's guidance when I'm lost,
A teacher who made something clear,
Their giving did not count the cost.

So I should bear in mind those deeds,
Which I must emulate to please
My fellowman, who has great needs,
For it's by giving we find ease.

The lifting of life's load can leave
Both weak and wise, weary and worn.
I'll not forget all those who gave
Support to me, since I was born.

Ann Nunan

Rain, Rain, Rain

Sometimes I think it never stops,
(The rain that is.)
The experts say it comes in drops,
But I don't think that's so.
I think that every day, or three
The world turns upside down,
And all the water in the sea
Falls back upon the ground.

J Feaviour

IN ANOTHER MAN'S WORLD

The past it was . . . 'tis dead and gone.
For some in the mind, it does live on.
A burden for sure the struggle is hard,
Living for today, paranoid always on guard.

Open the door of a soft spring morn,
Travel their path, look in their faces, see their scorn.
Their lips are pursed . . . eyes of stone,
'Tis not what they say . . . 'tis in their tone.

The banter was good in the local tonight,
Up to a point 'twas equal with no care nor spite.
Then the drink was heard to say, 'Not,'
As the landlord eased into, 'That's your lot.'

So another night ended as day had started,
Heart from soul from head tragically parted.
Lost long walk back to the house,
Mind the neighbours! Crash through the door
                          . . . quite as a mouse.

Davide A Bermingham

TORRENTIAL RAIN

Incessant rain,
Depression in tune with my mind,
Sombre black clouds low in the sky,
No end to my grief can I find!

Persisting storms,
Battering the defenceless shore,
Bring no solace to my despair,
And deep sorrow returns once more.

Throughout the land,
Many scenes of devastation,
And my black mood sinks to new depths.
Is this the end of creation?

Angry lightning,
Streaks across the dark autumn sky,
Crashing thunder shakes the building,
And flames destroy a house nearby!

Distant rumbling,
Will this violent storm subside?
As the depression moves away,
Despair ebbs away with the tide.

Peaceful silence,
Now my sorrow melts away,
As the sun brings a sign of hope,
And bravely I face a new day.

Gentle showers,
Bringing some occasional rain,
And my misery fades away,
As I learn to live once again!

Doreen M Bowers

Rain

Oh how I love the rain,
To feel the first drop of rain.
Fall upon your cheek.
Hear the pitter-patter on the ground,
To see it hit the windowpane.
Then watch it as it trickles down in lanes,
Walk along the street to see.
People hide under brollies deep.
They seem to think I am mad,
As I walk along the street,
As the rain comes pouring down.

Rose Mills

An Ode To 'The Yobbo'

You come in many guises, in leathers, suits or jeans,
You're singly unremarkable, you're broke or man of means.
You come in many sizes too, you're large or you are small,
When you're alone you quietly brood, you rarely smile at all.

But in a bunch of three or more; my God how you have changed,
You shout, you yell, you spoil and break, your behaviour is deranged.
You're a menace to society, a bully and you lack
The guts to stand up on your own, without your nauseous pack.

Yet when you're caught and bought to book, oh! aren't you sorry now?
You swear you will behave yourself, you'll honour any vow.
But just like any coward you tremble in the dock,
And when released on promises, our justices you mock!

You've got away with it again, you'll carry on with glee,
Why don't our courts just lock you up, and throw away the key?

In later years you're feeble, before long you'll be old,
Some 'yob' will kick your windows in and leave *you* in the cold.
Will you recall the misery, your thoughtlessness and spite,
Or will you sit and shiver, complaining of your plight?

My guess? You'll look for justice now, demand and make a fuss,
At last your past has caught you up . . . expect no help from *us*.

Andrew V Ascoli

Autumn Days

I saw a rabbit today
In a field where they'd cut the hay
When he saw me he ran away
I saw a rabbit today

I saw a fox today
He walked across the field where they'd cut the hay
He saw the rabbit run away
I saw a fox today

I saw a crow today
He scolded the fox in the field where they'd cut the hay
And watched the rabbit run away
I saw a crow today

I saw a farmer today
Working in the field where they'd cut the hay
He didn't see the crow, fox or rabbit run away
I saw a farmer today

I saw all these things today
In a field where they'd cut the hay
Now it's time to walk away
I saw all these things today

Allan McFadyean

THE LACK OF RAIN!

Go and clean the car Dad
You're bound to make it rain,
A rain dance round the water butt
Might fill it once again!

Go and clean the windows Mother
Rain spots might come to stain,
That cleaner man's gone long ago
And so's that bloomin' rain!

Reg Anderson

Untitled

My face is all scarred from my acne filled youth
The dentist is poised to remove my last tooth
I've been to the doctor, he told me to diet
And I had to admit my tummy's a sight
I've not seen my feet for quite some time
But it's quite a relief with feet like mine
I'd get nipped and tucked, I'd do it today
All stretched and sucked and lasered away
Now you might think I'm vain
But you don't know my plight
My nose has a bend, like Concord in flight
And my varicose veins, well what can I say?
I wear surgical stockings to keep them at bay
I've tried all the lotions and potions and creams
I've been to the gym on the running machines
Followed the videos, bought the books
But not a thing's improved my looks
So if beauty's skin deep
I have no doubt
I should have been born
With my skin inside out.

Trudy Simpson

TO DREAM THE DREAM

Happiness, to be
The one who makes a difference,
The salt of the earth.

Happiness, to have
Eyes to see God in others,
Jesus in disguise.

Happiness, to know
That giving my love away
Brings God's in return.

Happiness, to lift
My hands in prayer and always
Feel God's presence near.

Happiness, to dream
The dream God has for his world
Till it's my dream too!

Sheila E Harvey

HAPPINESS IS

Happiness is seeing
A face light up
After being sad
Happiness is saying
I love you
And they are glad
Happiness is seeing a child's face
Fill with joy
When giving a brand new toy
Happiness is being content
With life.

J Moore

Autumn Cheer

The weather's colder, the nights are drawing in,
Foliage and flora are getting rather thin.
Leaves are turning red and gold,
Lovely colours to behold.

Yellow leaves against the sky
Are very pleasing on the eye.
Russet nestling amongst the green
Is surely a sight that must be seen.

Swallows flying in formation,
Migrating to a warmer nation
To sit out the winter in a sunnier clime,
And come back just before summertime.

Walking briskly in the cold, crisp air,
Squirrels storing nuts in their winter lair;
A carpet of leaves covering the ground,
Their rustling makes a lovely sound.

Pine cones and conkers falling from up high,
Blackberries and apples baked in a pie.
Root veg and other food of the season,
We can look forward to autumn with good reason.

Kathy Rawstron

THE MEANING OF TRUE HAPPINESS

Happiness is being content with life
A person is able to accept their share of strain and strife
They do not go about each day complaining
Instead they accept their problems as a way of gaining
Gaining new knowledge as a problem is solved
Finding a quicker answer when other people are involved
Everyone can make another person's life much better
Whether it be by talking or by sending them a letter

Happiness for many is watching their daughter or son
Getting a good education and spending time with them in fun
All would like their children to grow up with good health
Which is far more important than a person's wealth
People can go to visit their granny or grandad
And come home and tell the family how good a time they had
It is a fact in life that it is the little things that count
Instead of a sum of money no matter what amount

Happiness for a person is being able to know
That if they are unwell there is somewhere they can
Go and speak to their minister or to one of the medical staff
Pour out their troubles and again be able to laugh
Another way of getting happy is speak to a true friend
A person who will stand by another always until the end
But always remember there is happiness and do not feel odd
This comes from the one above who is the almighty God

Robert Doherty

A Norfolk Landscape

I'm glad to be in Norfolk
Now that the summer's here.
With its plethora of wildlife
Pheasants, grouse and muntjac deer.

As I gaze through the window
What can I see?
A beautiful landscape
Laid out before me.

To the forefront a garden
Designed with such care.
With beds full of roses
Perfuming the air.

A gate in the trellis
Leads into a field,
Bright yellow with rape -
A bountiful yield.

This slopes down to a hollow
Where close by a stream
Lies the village of Bradenham
But few houses are seen.

Trees and fields surround it
On every side,
And form a haven of peace
Where folks can reside.

Away from the hustle
And bustle of the town,
This spells happiness for me
And where I'd love to settle down.

A M Craven

HAPPY HOLIDAYS!

In different surroundings
Under different skies
Feel the benediction
That in all things lies.

Bask in God's goodness
As you lie in the sun.
Everywhere see the beauty
Of the all-lovely One.

If you go a-sailing
O'er depths of ocean blue
Think that in depths of mercy
God hid your sins from view.

And if you should see mountains
Remember that your aid
Comes from the Creator
Who mighty mountains made.

Then satisfied with pleasant days
And all you've seen and done
Come back, come refreshed
From your holiday in the sun.

V M Archer

HAPPINESS IS . . .

An autumn wood
Crisp and cold,
Sun glinting through
Turning leaves gold.
Tails a-wagging
Dogs running free,
Rolling on grass
Barking with glee.
Throw a stick
Oh what fun,
Throw some more
Dogs love to run.
Tired at last
Time to go home,
Where happiness is . . .
A big, juicy bone.

Beryl M Malkin

FEELINGS

When you are sad and feeling low in a melancholy state
Your thoughts turn inwards to better times, images you create
You think of others less better off
Whose circumstances are really rough
And realise now what you did possess
Was a feeling one calls happiness

Possess it or lose it, give it or choose it
To get by without it is hard I admit
The voice of a loved one, a gentle caress
A thoughtful gesture I must confess
A devoted dog who wags his tail
Brings a happiness that does prevail

What other feelings can bring such pleasure
It glows, it shows the perfect treasure
So whatever makes you happy try to cultivate
By sharing it with others so they may participate

Barbara Tunstall

GOLF CRAZY

We stroll from the clubhouse,
We've paid the green fee,
So I'm feeling great
As we reach the first tee.

We toss for the honours,
My friend starts to curse,
I've won yet again . . .
So I'm teeing off first.

I take out my driver,
And survey the scene,
The long stretching fairway,
The lush distant green.

I place a new ball
On the white plastic tee,
I take a few swings,
Just to loosen the knee.

I take up my stance,
I swing back the club,
I've sliced the damn ball
Into thick looking scrub.

I've lost my new ball,
First shot of the day,
And things get worse
Every hole that I play.

We finish the round,
I'm miles over par,
I feel such a fool,
As we head for the bar.

We've had a few drinks,
I've stopped feeling shame,
As we get out our diaries . . .
To arrange our next game!

Dennis Young

Happiness Is . . .

Happiness is love, comfort and security,
freedom from care, hate and poverty.
It is to be able to meet all troubles with tranquillity.
Happiness is, for me, a primrose covered wood in spring.
Driving fast, alone, when I can sing, unheard, loudly,
Or quiet evenings spent with friends, talking.
Happiness is walking on high cliffs and watching the sea
fling mighty waves on granite rocks,
and be accompanied by dear friends laughing and free.
Happiness is fragile, handle it with care and guard it well,
give thanks for it, for you can never tell
how long it will hold you in its spell.

Lydia M Storey

The Betting Shop

Through the door to faraway places,
dogs at Romford, horses at Catterick,
the winners are there for the skilful to pick.
Study the form, fill out a slip
hand your money to the cashier, quick.
And wait for the 'off'.

The commentator with tripping tongue
expertly names each horse as it runs.
Together they're bunched for most of the race
then the favourite starts to lengthen the space
between him and the others, excitement is high
as horse after horse goes galloping by.

But now the grey finds extra pace,
and alongside the favourite takes up the chase
to the winning post, commentary voice getting higher
the grey flashes past to win at the wire.
One more crumpled betting slip falls to the floor,
joining the others thrown down before.

Gerard Chamberlain

ANOTHER WORLD

It's weird to think
What was there
Before our world
Was anywhere.
Just space I suppose,
Or maybe not.
Was it cold
Or was it hot?
There must have been life
In another place,
Another world,
Another space,
Another universe?
Light years away?
I wonder why
I'm here today.
Was the 'big bang'
Really true?
Did it create
Me and you?
Are there aliens
Out there now?
If so - where?
I wonder how.
Our Earth was formed
Long, long ago.
Was it different,
Unknown so?
Was it the world
We know today?
Was the style of living
Like our way?

I suppose I'll
Never understand
What it was like
Before this land.

Rosemary Mortimore

ANCHOR BOOKS
SUBMISSIONS INVITED
SOMETHING FOR EVERYONE

ANCHOR BOOKS GEN - Any subject, light-hearted clean fun, nothing unprintable please.

THE OPPOSITE SEX - Have your say on the opposite gender. Do they drive you mad or can we co-exist in harmony?

THE NATURAL WORLD - Are we destroying the world around us? What should we do to preserve the beauty and the future of our planet - you decide!

All poems no longer than 30 lines.
Always welcome! No fee!
Plus cash prizes to be won!

Mark your envelope (eg *The Natural World*)
And send to:
Anchor Books
Remus House, Coltsfoot Drive
Peterborough, PE2 9JX

OVER £10,000 IN POETRY PRIZES TO BE WON!

Send an SAE for details on our New Year 2003 competition!